LINDA BOZZO

AMAZING BEAKS

PowerKiDS
press™
New York

To my family and friends and all of your amazing features that make you who you are.
—LBS

Published in 2008 by The Rosen Publishing Group, Inc.
29 East 21st Street, New York, NY 10010

First Edition

Editor: Joanne Randolph
Book Design: Kate Laczynski
Photo Researcher: Nicole Pristash

Photo Credits: Cover, pp. 7, 9, 11, 13 Shutterstock.com; p. 5 © www.istockphoto.com/Michael Chlipek; p. 15 © www.istockphoto.com/Elijah Low; p. 17 © BIOS Klein & Hubert/Peter Arnold, Inc.; p. 19 © www.istockphoto.com/Rich Phalin; p. 21 © www.istockphoto.com/Warren Brooks.

Library of Congress Cataloging-in-Publication Data

Bozzo, Linda.
  Amazing beaks / Linda Bozzo. — 1st ed.
     p. cm. — (Creature features)
Includes index.
  ISBN 978-1-4042-4169-5 (library binding)
  1. Bill (Anatomy)—Juvenile literature. I. Title.
QL697.B69 2008
591.4'4—dc22
                                          2007025882

Manufactured in the United States of America

CONTENTS

SO MANY BEAKS!

What comes to mind when you think of beaks? Maybe you think of robins, owls, or blue jays. These are all animals that have a beak for a mouth. All beaks do not look the same. Most important, they do not all work the same. This is because an animal's beak is **adapted** to its **habitat** and the kind of food it eats.

Strong beaks squash hard nuts and seeds. Long beaks can reach fruit high up in tree branches. Some beaks are heavy. Others are light. Here is a peek at some amazing beaks!

The oddly shaped beak of the flamingo is specially suited to separate mud and other matter from the food it eats.

PLAYFUL TOUCANS

Chances are, you like to play. Well, toucans do, too. Toucans will sometimes toss fruit in the air and catch it in their beak. The toucan's colorful beak is very large. Its beak is also very light and has sharp, sawlike edges. The reason for the huge beak is not known. The toucan likes fruit best, but it will also eat lizards and other small animals.

When this colorful bird sleeps, it rests its beak over its back. A toucan will tuck its head under its wing and tail feathers to hide from **predators**. Goodnight!

The toucan's beak is so large that it is thought the bird may use it to scare enemies away. The beak may also help it reach fruit on tree branches.

A POWERFUL BEAK

The greenwing macaw has a strong beak. In fact, it is so strong it could snap a broomstick in half! It is no wonder this large parrot likes to chew. A macaw needs plenty of wood on which to chew. This keeps its beak in good shape.

The beak of this bird is very heavy and sharp. A macaw's beak is made to crush nuts and large seeds. Because of its beak, the macaw can cut into fruits and nuts that other animals cannot eat.

The greenwing macaw is a smart bird that can live over 75 years. Sometimes people keep these large, colorful birds as pets.

SHARP AS A KNIFE

There is no need to wonder what the oystercatcher likes to eat. Its name tells us! It feeds on oysters and other shellfish on coasts around the world.

Its long, strong orange beak is as sharp as a knife. An oystercatcher will use the sharp tip of its beak to force open the shell of an oyster or other shellfish. It may also smash the shell and then use its long beak to pick the meat out. Oystercatchers that hunt for food in sand or mud have a more pointed beak. They use it to find worms.

This American black oystercatcher uses its strong beak to pry, or force, open shells. Its beak is a natural wedge, which is a simple tool that helps push things apart.

A FISHING NET

Have you ever seen a pelican? The pelican has a cool beak. It is long and has a pouch underneath. A pelican uses its beak for many important jobs. It is helpful in building nests and keeping the pelican's feathers clean. It is also great for fishing. To fish, a pelican opens its large beak. Just like it is using a fishing net, this bird **scoops** up fish in its pouch. It will tip its beak high into the air and swallow the fish.

A pelican's beak has a **hook** at the end. This hook can kill **prey** or scare predators.

Pelicans will fish in groups by chasing fish into shallow water and then scooping them up with their beaks. Large fish are caught using the hook on the beak.

A BIRD WITH A HORN

Look, there is a rhinoceros in that tree! A rhinoceros hornbill, that is. The rhinoceros hornbill's name comes from the fact that it has a horn, called a casque, on its beak. Some think this casque makes the hornbill's call louder. It may also help the bird knock down fruit from the trees in its rain forest home.

The hornbill uses its beak to eat bugs, small animals, and fruit. When it is time to eat, the hornbill takes hold of the food. Then the hornbill throws its head back. The food slides down its throat.

The hornbill's huge beak is reddish orange at the base fading to white at the tip. The rhinoceros hornbill likes to eat figs best.

THAT'S NOT A BIRD!

Not every animal that has a beak is a bird. The platypus is a one-of-a-kind animal that has an amazing beak. It is not hard like a bird's beak. A platypus's beak is soft like rubber. The bill can feel the **electric fields** that are around all animals. This is a helpful skill since the platypus closes its eyes and ears when it swims!

It uses its bill almost like eyes as it swims and looks for prey. It can also swim and dive without bumping into things. It has its beak to thank for that!

Here you can see the platypus's wide, rubbery beak. The platypus makes its home in the rivers and streams of eastern Australia.

EATING WITH A SPOON

Have you ever heard of a bird eating with a spoon? Well, the spoonbill has a spoon built right into its beak!

To catch food, the spoonbill opens its beak. The spoonbill then swishes its beak back and forth in water that is not too deep. The spoon-shaped part of its beak can feel even very small movements. When it feels something, like a fish, move, it snaps its beak closed. If all goes well, the hungry bird will have caught its next meal. Time to eat!

The spoonbill is one of the many animals that find their food by touch. Spoonbills are also good at catching bugs with their long, flat beaks.

THE SMALLEST BIRD

The hummingbird is the smallest bird in the world. This bird pokes its pointed beak into flowers. It uses its **tongue** to suck out the **nectar**. A hummingbird's tongue is longer than its beak. Some hummingbirds have short beaks to reach into small flowers. Other hummingbirds have long beaks to reach deep into large flowers. A hummingbird also uses its small beak to catch insects and to make a nest for its young.

The hummingbird must eat a lot to live. It spends most of the day looking for and eating food. Luckily it has the perfect beak for the job!

Here you can see the hummingbird's thin, pointed beak. As it dips its beak into flowers, the bird beats its wings very quickly to let it float in one spot.

BEAKS ARE IMPORTANT

An animal's beak is important for many things. Beaks are used to build nests, to keep a bird's feathers clean, to talk to other animals, and more. The beak's main purpose is to help an animal find and eat food, though.

The shape and size of an animal's beak may help tell you what the animal eats and where it finds its food. Next time you see a bird or another animal with a beak, try to guess what it eats. Remember that these amazing beaks help keep many animals alive all over the world.

GLOSSARY

adapted (uh-DAPT-ed) Changed to fit requirements.

electric fields (ih-LEK-trik FEELDZ) The places around something that have the power to produce light, heat, or movement.

habitat (HA-beh-tat) The kind of land where animals or plants naturally live.

hook (HUK) Something that is curved at one end.

nectar (NEK-tur) A sweet juice found in flowers.

predators (PREH-duh-terz) Animals that kill other animals for food.

prey (PRAY) An animal that is hunted by another animal for food.

scoops (SKOOPS) Picks up as if with a spoon or shovel.

tongue (TUNG) A part inside the mouth used to eat, make sounds, and swallow.

INDEX

WEB SITES

Due to the changing nature of Internet links, PowerKids Press has developed an online list of Web sites related to the subject of this book. This site is updated regularly. Please use this link to access the list:

www.powerkidslinks.com/cfeat/beak/